The Truth about Acid

Exploring the LSD Compound and
All the Hallucinogenic and
Psychotherapy Properties

Alex Gibbons

Copyright © 2019 Alex Gibbons.

All rights reserved. No part of this publication may be reproduced, distributed or transmitted in any form or by any means, including photocopying, recording, or other electronic or mechanical methods, without the prior written permission of the publisher, except in the case of brief quotations embodied in critical reviews and certain other non-commercial uses permitted by copyright law.

Trademarked names appear throughout this book. Rather than use a trademark symbol with every occurrence of a trademarked name, names are used in an editorial fashion, with no intention of infringement of the respective owner's trademark. The information in this book is distributed on an "as is" basis, without warranty. Although every precaution has been taken in the preparation of this work, neither the author nor the publisher shall have any liability to any person or entity with respect to any loss or damage caused or alleged to be caused directly or indirectly by the information contained in this book.

1. What is LSD? 4
  LSD - mind-altering civilization 4
  An artificial compound coming from a natural source 7

2. The history and cultural influence of LSD 9
  Short historic timeline of LSD 10
  The cultural revolution and Mckenna's take on LSD 14

3. The science behind LSD 20
  Chemistry of LSD 20
  Pharmacology of LSD 21

4. The effects of LSD 23

5. The therapeutic potential of LSD 27
  Studies 30
  Microdosing 32

6. Pros and cons of LSD 34

7. The similarities and differences between LSD, Psilocybin Mushrooms, MDMA & DMT 38

8. The future of LSD 43

9. LSD - the psychedelic remedy of the modern man 48

1. What is LSD?

LSD - mind-altering civilization

LSD is the prime substance that ignited the modern wave of interest towards psychedelics and the revolution of consciousness of world-wide proportions. The impact of lysergic acid on the human culture is unprecedented, as it not only boosted a mass appeal towards mind-altering compounds, but it also brought in mainstream forgotten aboriginal cultures and their knowledge of medicinal rituals with trance plants.

Therefore, we could say that LSD turned the page, expanding people's drive for enlightenment practices, as well as for a completely different approach to reality. With the experience of LSD, the practical industrialized society was beginning to search for meaning in the fantastic and symbolic realms.

The times synchronized perfectly such as to confer the optimal context for the LSD wave to emerge. In a social atmosphere affected by the recently passed World Wars, with the industrial revolution on the rise and the other smaller yet tormenting wars, like the Vietnam War, maintaining a status quo of general conflict and pressure, a shock that would shatter the conventional and bring new intelligence in the game was most welcomed.

The hippie movement offered fertile grounds for the culture of psychedelics to grow into a veritable culture. Peace and enlightenment were sought for in Eastern spirituality, as well as in the instant effect of psychedelic drugs and further on in South America's rituals of healing and spirit connection.

Lysergic acid funnels the bonding with nature but, at the same time, is a synthetic compound and thus could be seen as the link between the contemporary mechanized society and Mother Earth. As other psychedelics, it amplifies the senses and expands the area of perception in that you see more, hear more, and feel intense detail. This is partly the source of fascination towards the world and life overall that one remains with as an aftereffect of LSD.

The sensation is that you are perceiving the divine and, at the same time, being conscious of its presence within. This is a truly revolutionary mindset in the context of the traditionalist society that survived a world crisis and was brought, with the aid of psychedelics, in the middle of the modern renaissance.

It was LSD that sparked the appetite for the unknown realities of the hallucinogenic states, because acid was something very different. It induced a sort of lightness of being instead of the, more often than not, heavy trip of the magic mushrooms or the other psychotropic plants that usually provoked a trance.

Furthermore, LSD had a more digital effect. It didn't present the usual hallucinations of mythical animals, fairies, monsters, or whatever creatures dwelled in the collective imaginarium. Its effect was to reveal the image of vibrations, the vibration of sound and light that received form, as well as objects that were seemingly inanimate, like rocks or furniture.

It was thus opening the eyes to the life that inherently is in everything, infusing the reality that we all perceive in a similar way with spirit. For all these reasons, LSD was the perfect substance to attract and awaken the enthusiasm.

The consumerist trend, in part, diluted the initial revelations, as with the advance in the discovery and research of psychotropic substances, a great number of psychedelic acids emerged and were brought into the market. Different types of acids soon became recreational party drugs, the next generation changing the purpose of use, as well as the essential meaning behind the experience this substance induced.

Nonetheless, the tribal gatherings of today are marked by the feeling of communion between people and a profound connection with nature, the blueprints of the original psychedelic experience and the powerful collective insights that were the gift of LSD.

In addition, lysergic acid is in the midst of a new revival, since the recent medical studies have exposed its therapeutic potential and accustomed its use to the system of efficiency and alert rhythm characterizing our current society by introducing microdosing. This method of consuming LSD became popular in a short while, being the optimal solution for busy people.

An artificial compound coming from a natural source

Despite the fact that LSD's most usual presentation is on small paper stamps that have been soaked in the substance, its source is natural. Lysergic acid is extracted from a fungus that develops on rye seeds. In other words, it's the rot of a type of cereal that produces this mind-bending effect on human consciousness. Of course, one cannot consume the rotten rye and expect to have anything else but poisoning.

In support of this idea, there are several incidents that have been registered in the course of history, one of which is famous: the intoxication of an entire village in the 50's in France with the addled flour that the sole baker of the place had used to make bread for the population. The event is chronicled, but the circumstances in which such a large mass of people were poisoned are still unelucidated, especially as the effects were horrific and ended up with loss of human lives. Nonetheless, this type of event has added another dimension to the mythical image of the substance, more so as the intoxicated men presented the effects of strong hallucinations.

From another point of view, LSD presents yet another set of peculiarities: it is taken in very small doses of 100-400 micrograms, which means the extraction has to be highly diluted. It can penetrate the skin barrier and enter the bloodstream directly, lasting anywhere from 4-6 hours, where the experience is so powerful that its aftereffects can be sensed weeks, months, and even a year later.

When talking about LSD's effect of opening a gate towards interconnectivity with nature, with everything and everybody, with the universe, we should mention that this is, in fact, the action that this substance has on the neurons of the brain. It is like turning on the light in the neural network, freeing and activating all circuits. An enhancement in perception and a leap of consciousness are only natural results of these processes.

For this reason, the notion that LSD alters the mind doesn't seem to grasp fully its encompassing influence, for the state of awareness is not bent but rather more comprehensive, present, and dynamic. Its effect is one of resetting the pre-existent predicament in which the brain functions, giving a restart to all connections and inducing a full-power operating mode.

Subsequently, it's for these incredible abilities that lysergic acid is studied as a therapeutic solution for a number of mental conditions, such as addiction, depression, anxiety, and post traumatic stress disorder (PTSD).

2. The history and cultural influence of LSD

Prior to LSD's synthesization, there have been documented cases of poisoning with rye and wheat that have gone bad. Lysergic acid is naturally occurring in ergot, a by-product of the infection with a fungus that turns the kernels of the cereals black. One of its horrific effects, if eaten, results in the rotting of the person's limbs and their subsequent coloring, turning them black.

In one circumstance around 1700, a family was poisoned and died, whereas around the mid-twentieth century in France, a whole village was intoxicated; several people died while others remained marked for life with severe physical and mental conditions. In all cases, apart from the rapid decay of the flesh, there were other symptoms that resemble much more what we know about LSD today, vivid hallucinations and delusions.

Given the combined effect that the ergot fungus had on the human body, as well as the abnormal, unassumed context in which this happened, the behavior of those inflicted was rather strange and violent. To add to this myth, there is a theory that states the famous Salem witch trials were a consequence of such poisoning of the population, during a highly rainy, wet summer that favoured the development of the fungus on the cereal used as food.

Although we are more or less discussing the same chemical compound, our firm knowledge of lysergic acid begins with the Swiss chemist Albert Hoffman on his bicycle ride home. It spans over a very short period compared to other psychedelics that have been used for millennia, defining the modern era of substances.

Short historic timeline of LSD

Albert Hoffman was researching a substance that would aid pregnant women with uterine contractions during childbirth. He synthesized the compounds from the ergot, obtaining a long list of lysergic acid derivatives, of which LSD was the 25th, hence its original naming as LSD-25.

This happened in 1938, but as he didn't find anything that seemed to be useful for his purpose, he put all the research in a drawer and left it on standby. It wasn't until 1943, when he thought he'd give it another shot, that he sent the substance to the pharmacological department for analysis.

Before doing this, Hoffman resumed the process of synthesizing, and the magical error occurred when a very small drop accidently fell on his skin. He went on without noticing the incident, but at a certain point during the work, he noticed that he was 'affected by a remarkable restlessness, combined with a slight dizziness' that compelled him to take the day off and go home (as he confesses in his book 'LSD, My Problem Child').

The aforementioned famous bicycle ride follows, and then, once in the intimacy of his house, he calmly gives off to the pleasant sensation of intoxication that was inducing a dreamlike state in which his imagination ran vividly, producing the now all-familiar visual patterns of kaleidoscopic pictures, mandalas, and distortions of vibration. This was the first trip on LSD that a human being had experienced, and it lasted about two hours.

The experience sparked his interest, so he submitted the compound to his laboratory at Sandoz to inquire further, carrying out tests on animals that would define its toxicity, tolerance, and other properties. The research continued with studies of its effects on human beings in a psychiatric environment, on schizophrenic and healthy individuals that, even though came out with no specific result in terms of therapeutic benefits, still remained a substantial promise.

The similarity of its effects with certain types of psychosis was the point of attraction for the psychiatrists that experimented further to establish its influence, but no evident correlation was determined. Nonetheless, during the '50s and '60s, LSD was the prime drug used in hallucinogenic assisted therapy. A great volume of documentation was produced in the medical research of lysergic acid, and over 40,000 people were prescribed this substance for therapeutic purposes.

The amazing effect that LSD had on the human brain generated a wave of enthusiasm among a different group of people, particularly among the brilliant minds of the day that were rather interested in its influence on consciousness. Starting with the psychologist Timothy Leary, who eventually became the star of the psychedelic revolution, a series of cultural personalities were invited to take part in assisted LSD experiments and afterwards to share and spread the insights they were granted.

These were the first steps that were taken by the elite of the pre-hippie period and the most important basis for the new consciousness revival that was to take up the whole world. Leary was prophesying 'Turn on, tune in, and drop out', words that would become a meme of the counterculture rising in those moments in the USA and spreading across the globe as a response to the pre-established blueprint of reality that was getting too tight and abusive for a generation of enlightened spirits.

At the same time, the secret services around the world were indulging in all sorts of mind control experiments, using with predilection amphetamines and mescaline. In this type of pursuit, the CIA started its research LSD as part of the controversial work performed by the Project MKULTRA, inquiring on its capacity to become some sort of truth serum.

Under the umbrella of top-secret operations, lysergic acid was administered to hundreds of men, including military employees and agents, as well as individuals from the general public, especially from the disadvantaged layers of society, like homeless people, prostitutes or delinquents, of which most were given the substance without knowledge or consent. It was a wild type of research that evidently produced no solid results apart from the terrorizing of those individuals, and the project officially ended in the mid 1970s.

Under these predicaments and inflated by the overall hype of the hippie movement, the use of LSD peaked in the 60s and 70s, transforming into a veritable hysteria. A veil of unconsciousness dominated the consumption of LSD during that period, and although there was a powerful trend involving awareness and enlightenment, there were numerous cases of people taking lysergic acid in contexts and settings that were definitely unfavorable, ending in nervous collapses, violent accidents, criminality, and suicide. All of these events were, of course, exploited by the media, damaging the public image of LSD and instating this substance as a dangerous drug.

Consequently, in 1970, LSD was declared a Schedule I drug with high potential for abuse and wasn't accepted for further research into its therapeutic benefits. This decision would halt the study of lysergic acid for many years in the USA, as well as in other parts of the world.

As of the 1980s, however, the interest reemerged in the recreational usage of LSD, as well as in the science of its therapeutic properties, and studies on its beneficial influence were resumed by newly formed organizations, such as MAPS (the Multidisciplinary Association of Psychedelic Studies) and The Beckley Foundation.

LSD is still popular among young people who consume it for amusement, but more so within ceremonial tribal gatherings that define the current new-age movement and individuals engaged in a personal pursuit of therapy or consciousness discovery. As for the medical scene nowadays, the interest in LSD is concentrated on its use in micro doses to support therapy.

The cultural revolution and Mckenna's take on LSD

All public figures that raised the idea to promote the spectacular effects that psychedelics had on the dynamics of the human brain were constantly persecuted; Timothy Leary, the father of the LSD movement, spent many years of his life in jail. The whole psychedelic culture ended up discredited by the media and oppressed by laws. Nonetheless, its aficionados were not only the hippies or, later on, the ravers, but an entire palette of individuals that one would surely not consider drug abusers.

They were scientists, business men, artists, people working in IT, politicians, doctors, and the list could go on indefinitely, citing people that led normal lives and actively participated in society. The enlightenment was there for anybody who had the courage and curiosity to delve into it. Moreover, in time, as the '60's revolutionary spirit mellowed, the psychedelics received a different glow, a more science-infused image that shed the conflict with establishment issues and established their presentation as guides to the subtle realms of reality and towards self-discovery and self-therapy.

Terence Mckenna inherited the legacy of Timothy Leary and further promoted the culture of psychedelics into the new era. He had entered the movement with a wild and essential step, praising the influence of magic mushrooms in our culture. In fact, the widespread consumption of psychedelic mushrooms is almost in its whole attributed to Terence and Dennis Mckenna, who developed a method to grow Stropharia cubensis, a type of mushroom that he became acquainted with in Colombia and introduced in mass to USA.

But more than developing a practical guide that supported the in-house growing of the mushrooms, he came up with a theory that stated they were, in fact, magical entities that had an essential role in the development of human culture over millennia and the evolution of our species. He was thus portraying psychedelics as a primordial element for human growth, one that was there with us all along and that was necessary and only natural to inquire further.

In Mckenna's opinion, going through life without psychedelics would resemble a life without sex. This was because the psychedelic compounds were the source of knowledge, of the laws that govern reality and the cosmos, the main source of novelty throughout our history, through the different types of plants people practiced with in all cultures of the globe. His approach was merging the tribal consciousness and know-how with the modern technologies and visions of the future.

With a degree in shamanism and ecology, Mckenna believed that bridging the old and new worlds was the key to a complete vision of humanity in which the missing evolutionary link that everybody was searching for was to be found in psychedelics. The door to understanding the ancient past civilizations, the meaning of life and means to make a sense out of the universe lay in entheogens.

Most fascinatingly, the psychedelic substances were leading to an enhanced system of perception in which the purest religious experience was the same thing as the encounter with pagan mythological characters and, at the same time, with the most bewildering science fiction scenarios.

What led him to the intense and exhaustive study of psychedelic substances and experiences was not the recreational use of drugs but the interest in the variety of religious experiences and different ways in which to grasp the understanding of human consciousness.

Aldous Huxley's book 'The doors of Perception' was, for Mckenna, the introduction into the wild world of the collective imaginarium, and from that moment, he started to develop his theory of the necessity and imminence of an archaic revival, a rebirth of the lost knowledge of human civilizations, those that went extinct along with the tribal counterpart that, although in a symbolic manner, kept the information well-hidden in their traditions. He believed these essential insights could and should be accessed through psychedelic experiences.

The first time Mckenna took acid was in 1965, a batch produced by Sandoz, in a dose of 500 micrograms, which is a serious quantity, rapidly expelling all preconceived ideas that one retains in terms of what's real and what's not. His words on this initial experience: 'It was a whole universe that polarized itself into two concepts. One was like God - it was profound. It was that organ tone in the Bach B minor Mass (...) then the other thing was hilarious and absurd and it caused me to bust up hysterically for long minutes. I spent an hour and a half in this place just ricocheting between things so awesome that I felt like a flea in God's bedroom.'

But Mckenna confesses that he appreciates LSD in its whole potential only when he combines it with hashish because, by itself, lysergic acid is not the type of substance to produce mind-blowing visions with flying dragons or his beloved 'elf machines' that dwelled in the high realms mastered by DMT.

LSD is only enhancing the perception of reality and, of course, leaving your imagination free to encounter whatever beings from outer space you'd wish to meet, but it does not force the introduction of such mystical guides. It's only you in the LSD trip; your consciousness is your sole guide, contrary to psilocybin, ayahuasca, or other plant entheogens that are always accompanied with a specific guide to take you on an insightful journey. In other words, Mckenna was in the search of mythological and science-fiction fairy tales, and the only way he could satisfy his need with LSD was to combine it with generous doses of hashish.

For Mckenna, the exploration of psychedelics is a way to prepare yourself for death, a means through which you go past the limits of the event horizon into the great unknown through the deepest meditation process one is able to induce while still alive.

Terence Mckenna was one of the world's greatest visionaries, the one who introduced the term 'psychonaut' to define the explorers of consciousness and recuperate this holy pursuit from the shame of the public opinion that denigrated its purpose, considering it mere addiction.

He died of a brain tumour that, despite the rumors, could've been the effects of a life-long consumption of drugs, but as doctors told him, was only nature and its intricate ways of messing with people lives. He spent his last days answering the thousands of fan emails and contemplating the mysteries of life and death, something he did during his entire existence.

3. The science behind LSD

Chemistry of LSD

LSD is, in chemical terms, lysergic acid diethylamide, part of the great family of indole alkylamines, including tryptamines, such as psilocin, the active substance in magic mushrooms, or N,N-dimethyltryptamine or DMT. LSD is found on blotters, stamp-like pieces of paper submerged in acid, microdots, or small tablets and dissolved in solutions of water or alcohol.

Lysergic acid is synthesized from the ergot, the fungus of the rye, called C. purpurea, and its chemical appearance is that of a tetracyclic ring ($C_{20}H_{25}ON_3$). A number of homologs and derivatives have been studied, but none has been found to be as potent as LSD. One of its most familiar siblings is LSA, the substance extracted from the seeds of the Morning Glory.

The regular dosage is between 100 and 400 micrograms. A dose of 25 micrograms is expected to ignite visible effects when consumed, but the moderate dosage that would allow the full spectrum of potential is 75-150 micrograms.It alters perception by infusing the person with a state of euphoria and promoting one's inner capacity for introspection and for discerning the hypnagogic coordinates and dreams.

One may experience pseudo-hallucinations, so-called because they are not visions of non-existing characters and events but enhancements of perception of external stimuli that are there in reality. Synesthesia and the distortion of the time and space dimension describes what people may be tempted to define as illusion.

Pharmacology of LSD

One hypothesis that explains the effects of LSD on the human consciousness is that the brain experiences an informational overload of the senses. The usual functioning mode of our mind to select the needed sensory information and thus avoid overload of unnecessary stimuli and redundant information simply does not have a path to be transferred from reception to cognition.

The apparatus that performs the selection of perceived information is the thalamus, , a ball of neurons in the center of our brain that decides what is relevant for us to know and what should be neglected from our exterior environment. LSD enables the thalamus to do its job properly; thus, a great wave of information penetrates the mind, pushing the brain into an overwhelming state in which it has to deal with greater input coming from its senses. This state of overload is what we decipher as a psychedelic state of mind.

Moreover, LSD has been found to interfere with the production of serotonin, and it's believed this neurotransmitter is also influencing the thalamus, interfering with the function of selecting the proper information from the outside medium. To study if serotonin is a key factor of the cortex overload, Katrin H. Peller from the University Hospital for Psychiatry Zurich experimented with a substance that would block the serotonin receptors.

The research was done on subjects that were administered LSD and ketanserin, the respective blocker. The results were surprising, as the people who were given this duo did not present the usual psychedelic effects of the acid. Further, the conclusions of the experiment stated that, by impeding the thalamus from performing the process of selection, awareness is shifted to a specific part of the brain, which is the posterior cingulate cortex.

Other studies revealed that LSD resets the pre-existing neural connections by creating new branches between neighboring cells, or in other words, greatly enlarging the number of pathways the brain uses when perceiving and disseminating the exterior information, as well as its capacity to reorganize the information that's already in the memory.

4. The effects of LSD

The LSD trip lasts 6-12 hours, depending on the dosage and the intensity of the journey. The live memory of the state lingers for weeks after, while the after-effect of a powerful LSD experience can be sensed throughout the rest of your lifetime.

The overstimulation of the senses that results in a general overload of the brain alters the normal perception of reality, enhancing emotions and producing an overwhelming avalanche of thoughts. This is the cause of the impression of hallucinating, where you think you see things that are not there when you're merely getting far more impressions from the existing reality. With this ultra-sensibilization, the information coming from the senses is often misinterpreted, and in some cases, the senses become confused, producing a state of synesthesia, where sounds produce forms and forms have different tastes.

The world appears in much more vivid colors, vibrations become visible, shapes get distorted, sometimes morphing one from another, and halos of light give the impression that you can discern the auras of things and beings. Hearing is also highly augmented; therefore, people consuming LSD testify to hearing sounds with more acuity, from a long distance and with a definition that allows great many details to penetrate the perception barrier.

Although one may experience a rapid shift in moods, the general state is one of euphoria, with dream-like experiences in an atmosphere of overall awareness and peacefulness. When the brain is totally overwhelmed, it's natural sometimes to become stuck in old mental patterns and refuse the experience, in which case the whole trip takes a turn towards confusion and ultimately anxiety. This scenario is the one of a classical bad trip that you can only avoid by freeing your mind of the usual expectations.

By inducing this altered sense of perception, lysergic acid messes with one's capacity to recognize and understand reality. One of the most often met consequences is a detachment from the self, by separation from your old belief system. This is what defines a transcendental experience in which time appears as a continuum, cold and hot are regarded as mere states of being, the borders between what seems to be a dream and what was, until that moment, stable reality, dissolves.

The feeling is of profound merging with everything that is within, comprising yourself and everything that lies outside, constituting the external environment. The dissolution of the self turns into a sense of community with oneself, as well as with everything there is. Peace, forgiveness, compassion, and an overwhelming sensation of unconditional love are the feelings a person on LSD experiences and the ultimate definition of a spiritual awakening.

Interfering with the levels of serotonin in the body, LSD is directly influencing the perception and behavior of the person, as well as the regulatory systems, such as hunger, temperature, motor control, and sexuality. But it goes even further by having a powerful impact on the emotional dimension of the individual: one can feel several emotions at the same time and swing rapidly from one emotional state to another. The confusion of senses, perception, and the emotional overrun could be disconcerting for some.

The effects of LSD linger on when the trip is finished, maintaining its memory through the recurrence of flashbacks. The after-effects are the increase of confidence, appetite for life, and focus on what is truly meaningful for one's being, thus generating important decisions and concrete changes in the long term. LSD also eliminates or considerably reduces addiction by revealing that we don't really need such attachments to clarify one's purpose in life.

We can also talk about the effects of a bad trip that erupt, as mentioned above, when one refuses to shift its pre-existing stand-point and actually accept the trip that LSD proposes. In these cases, panic, paranoia, and psychosis are waiting in line. As an after-effect, it can degenerate into a state of strong fatigue, aching body and muscles, insomnia, and depression, but this is only the consequence of not being able or open enough to assume the greatness of reality and existence.

These are also the fallouts of treating this powerful psychedelic substance with disrespect and mixing it with other drugs like amphetamines or alcohol. Also, not paying attention to the most important principle of 'set and setting' can severely disrupt your journey. The ambiance of a club or an environment of noise, agitation, crowds, unfamiliar grounds, and unfamiliar people, a context that is provoking anxiety are not the proper settings for a peaceful and insightful LSD trip. In the same line of thought, the interior setting is as important, whereas a state of mind of confusion, depression, or nervousness is not a fertile medium for enlightenment or a firm basis for self-discovery.

A regular intake of LSD creates tolerance that makes users increase the dosage; however, a break of a short period generally solves the problem. A typical LSD trip is so powerful, however, that one generally needs a few months to integrate the insights and implement the beneficial understandings in their daily routine and in the dynamic of their life.

5. The therapeutic potential of LSD

Due to LSD's capacity to induce special states of mind in which the person is faced with a powerful feeling of interconnection, as well as profound spiritual experiences, this substance is seen as a reliable solution for helping people that deal with life-threatening illnesses or conditions and that suffer from anxiety. The after-effects of using LSD support these purposes by promoting one's self-confidence, personal growth, belief systems, and confidence.

The manner in which LSD, as well as other psychedelics, work is by restructuring the brain, addressing particularly the dysfunctional mental patterns and the ideas and emotions that aren't in congruence with the rest of your being. The feeling of interconnectivity and union, as reflected within, is the catalyzer of containing the whole of yourself and thus accepting yourself for who you are, addressing your problems with courage, honesty and compassion, and maintaining an attitude of clarity and peace. LSD is promoting an uplifting perspective on life and a healthy approach of the individual path, which sustains the process of cleansing and renewal. In this course, issues and features that are unnecessary are eliminated; the burdens transform into practical tasks that, once resolved, give way to ease and freedom.

The feeling of communion is also associated with the sensation of detachment from the ego. One feels united with every atom of the universe and, by this, is freed from the attachment to his rigid system of beliefs, as well as to his specific problems. This is a natural consequence of being compelled to see the definition of the cosmos, the grand picture in all its complexity, instead on focusing exclusively on your own universe. You could say you have the opportunity to experience your smallness in the greatness of the universe.

The current research and experimental trials that are conducted to determine LSD's therapeutic abilities are based on the preliminary studies from the 1950-1960 period, when lysergic acid was considered helpful in the treatment of addiction, PTSD, depression, and anxiety. The procedure is to administer LSD to the patient while the therapist takes the role of the shaman, who guides and confers a feeling of comfort and security, while addressing the cause of his problems, the motif that ultimately sent him to therapy in the first place.

Under LSD, the patient is in an altered state of consciousness in which he can easily access his true self and work on his persona if the right instruments are found or handed to him. The experience has the form of a dream or trance that is greatly infused with symbolism and the figures of the unconscious, but at the end, the work that's been done has tremendous effects. Despite the way we forget dreams and despite the experience of other psychoactive substances, such as DMT, you will probably remember every detail of the LSD trip, a feature that enhances the benefits of such a journey.

Today, therapists, self-proclaimed, non-conventional, or with traditional degrees, are pursuing therapy with LSD, giving lysergic acid to their patients to treat their medical conditions or aid their personal development pursuit. Although not legal, these people play the roles of the modern urban shamans, performing their work with perseverance and a great dose of awareness, promoting their practice by word of mouth from one satisfied patient to the other.

Most of them have normal jobs and live a normal life, and there's no evident reason to suspect something from their appearance or their overall behavior. The current laws, however, would punish such actions severely, as LSD is considered dangerous for abuse, so giving LSD to others would almost be an act of violence. Moreover, the social predicament is as unfriendly with such therapies, for the media took care to portraitize acid as a cause of numerous accidents, delinquency and crimes, as part of the denigration campaign of the 'war on drugs'. Nonetheless, there are more and more people that take part in such private sessions with lysergic acid, people that are suffering from different conditions or in pursuit of discovery and spirituality as seen from a non-conventional point of view.

Studies

To this day, the research and experimental trials that have been done concerning the use of LSD as medicine for a number of mental conditions are still too few and, in some aspects, inconclusive enough to funnel the therapeutic implementation on a mass scale. Most materials were produced during the 50s, 60s, 70s, and it's only recently that the active interest of conventional medicine towards lysergic acid has reemerged.

The long period of pause due to the legal restraints made it even harder to regroup and restart the clinical investigations of LSD. Nonetheless, there is sufficient evidence to bring LSD into therapy again, more so in the cases where the pressure of time makes the difference, such as terminal stages of illnesses, because the beneficial effects of the therapy with LSD are manifesting immediately, but existing therapeutical means need a lot longer to produce relevant transformations in the patient's life.

A study conducted in London by R. Carhart-Harris, M. Kaelen, M. Bolstridge, T. Williams, L. Williams, R. Underwood, D. Nutt, titled 'The paradoxical psychological effects of lysergic acid diethylamide (LSD)' (2016) concluded that LSD could offer a promising treatment for depression and anxiety. The experimentation was performed on healthy individuals that were given a single dose of LSD, and the results showed the experience provided them with an after-effect of optimism, openness, and an uplifted mood for up to two weeks after the session.

A similar study by T. Krebs and P-O Johansen, termed 'LSD for alcoholism' (2012), addressed the problem of alcohol addiction and the beneficial results. People that participated in this trial exhibited the same feeling of optimism and a boost of confidence that conferred the necessary power to face their alcohol problem and deal with it on a psychological, as well as practical, level.

Furthering Mckenna's view of LSD as a means to get acquainted with death, ultimately challenge and make peace with this primordial fear, research has been done in the quest of alleviating the anxiety of people that were dealing with terminal diseases. Among the studies performed in this sector, there is one very compelling trial conducted by P. Gasser,
K. Kirchner, T. Passie, 'LSD-assisted psychotherapy for anxiety associated with a life-threatening disease: A qualitative study of acute and sustained subjective effects' (2015). It visibly reduced the level of anxiety produced by the fear of dying, not only by introducing them to the unknown, but also by supporting relaxation and improving their strength and ability to cope with the ending of life as they know it. The inquiry registered the after-effects lasting for a period of about a year.

There are also reports from celebrities that participated in LSD therapy, such as Cary Grant, the famous movie star, who was one of the first to be treated with lysergic acid. He did the therapy in 1958, taking one hundred doses over a period of three years. His testimony is that LSD helped him resolve childhood traumas and difficult relationship issues that he'd been carrying around for a lifetime. Acid brought him peace, the power of acceptance, and clarity of vision.

Microdosing

The hype of the moment is microdosing psychedelics, and LSD is preeminently leading the way. This method of using acid fits perfectly with today's society that lives in a highly alert rhythm and is in the search of remedies that would not impede their activity or produce a shock that could slow them down, make them lose focus, and make them less efficient. The interesting fact is that, in microdoses, LSD is helpful especially in those aspects, bringing on clarity and productivity.

Microdosing is done with 10 micrograms every fourth day, as prescribed by its pioneer James Fadiman. The usual effects of LSD are not apparent when using this method as the dose is too small to produce any type of sensible sensation. But its after-effects, on the other hand, can be sensed starting with day two and are manifested through a set of positive changes in behavior and state of mind, including the power of concentration, an uplifted mood, a boost in energy that generates productive activity, clarity and balance, and enhanced sense of confidence.

The medical research on microdosing is extremely scarce, but the internet is abundant with stories from people that have pursued this type of treatment, and their testimonies are extremely positive. Moreover, the microdosing craze has just begun.

6. Pros and cons of LSD

As you've seen by now, there's a variety of ways in which a person can consume LSD. Therefore, the benefits and negative aspects depend on the purpose with which you take the drug. It is evident that it depends greatly whether you use LSD therapeutically, in a process of healing or growing yourself, or just to have fun one night at a party.

As a general rule, psychedelics are substances that generate an introspective process in which you travel within, so they are to be taken in environments that offer the necessary intimacy to be free to go along with the trip. When you get interrupted by the exterior realm or are in the pressure of maintaining your focus outside yourself, it is most likely that you will get stressed and respond negatively to that stimuli.

The state of being when on LSD is susceptible to changes and getting disrupted is reflected in the overall harmony of the trip. You are also highly empathic and feeling all vibrations from outside manifesting strongly inside yourself. For this reason, the environments with big crowds and agitated spirits would most likely provoke tension within you; taking a trip and going for a walk on a busy street would be like going to the circus for the first time.

We discussed earlier the problem of set and setting, outlining that it is highly important to choose the proper ambience and enter a state of mind in which you are prepared for the journey, because it actually makes the difference between a good and a bad trip. LSD is an incredibly relative drug, so when facing anxiety or panic attacks, being under pressure for whatever reason, tired or troubled, nervous or agitated, it would be wise to postpone the trip because its effect would be immensely influenced.

Furthermore, it comes down to compatibility. The experience of LSD is inevitably astounding for everybody that tries it, but for some, it is so pleasurable and useful that they engage in a regular therapy or self-therapy, while for others, it's too disruptive to do it again. As such, it is a matter of your psychological and emotional structure, of acceptance and flexibility.

So, apart from the potential of a bad trip, there is no real con. But this doesn't mean you have to underestimate a bad trip as its after-effects can be devastating and long term. Mental conditions and past traumas can be healed with LSD therapy, but they can also be aggravated when the consumption is unconscious, unguided, or unprepared. A weak, unsure, and troubled person can be seriously affected, and the inability to face and control the manifestation of the effects and aftereffects of the trip can be tormenting, rooting the individual even more into their problems.

On the other hand, it is only when we truly face our fears and suffering that we become free and are able to reach above the surface of our issues, and LSD is evidently a great support in this direction. But for such beneficial, life-changing results, you need courage, perseverance, or the proper guide who knows what they're doing.

One of the biggest risks of taking LSD today is when buying it on the street and not from a reliable source that can attest to its purity. There's a high chance you'd not be given lysergic acid but another strain. There are a plethora of derivatives and other types of substances and psychedelic compounds that, from a chemical point of view, are considered acids but not LSD exactly. LSD is the most famous and the purest of them all, and due to this, there are many occasions when other types of substances are sold under its name.

The reasons are multiple, yet it's most likely that they're easier to produce and use cheaper ingredients and equipment. Most frequent acids that are passed on as LSD are Shulgin's recipes 2CI, 2CE, and 2CB. Even though they're definitely rougher, they do have an enlightening aspect if you manage to get through the first stages of pure madness and surrender your attachments to any fixed structures of perception.

Unfortunately, there is a list of other acids that you would never want to try, and you can stumble upon them anywhere, hidden in the same presentation as LSD, minuscule stamps with beautiful colorful prints on them. So, if you're not taking part in a clinical therapy with this substance, in a medical institution that is practicing this type of treatment or trials, it would be advisable to make sure your or your guide's source is trustworthy.

Moreover, when dealing with psychedelics, you become more aware of the energy that comes with the particular substance you consume. Some experienced users have even said they can feel the energy of the one who made the acid and the people that handled it before it got to them. Even if you don't have such a holistic approach to the experience, you can admit that it makes a difference if you were given LSD by a friendly, loving person or a nasty dealer.

As for toxicity, an LSD trip is as toxic as an aspirin, and this says a lot not only about its purity, but also about its general compatibility with the human organism.

7. The similarities and differences between LSD, Psilocybin Mushrooms, MDMA & DMT

These are the four main candidates for psychedelic therapy today used in a few traditional clinics in medical environments by unauthorized guides and urban shamans that take you in nature or in a pleasant interior, and probably most of all in self-therapy by people who pursue self-development, self-healing, creative inspiration, or spiritual endeavors. Each is very different than the other, but all of them are used to treating the main mental conditions affecting our contemporary society: depression, anxiety, PTSD, and addiction. In this sense, one could notice the paradox of these truly helpful substances that are used under hiding and more often than not in party contexts where they are unconsciously abused, as well as the irony of being under the restrictment of the law.

Apart from magic mushrooms, which are the fruits of mother nature, the other three are chemical compounds synthesized in labs from a number of sources. This has a profoundly distinct effect on the nature of the trip, in which the natural medicinal substances inducing hallucinations, trance, or any other psychedelic experiences are said to come with a spirit guide. The sensation is as if the drug's spirit enters your being and gets a grip on you, guiding your journey and grounding you at the same time, although the feeling is sometimes so strong that it can become unbearable unless you release the control and thus free yourself.

With the magic mushrooms, this feeling, as if you sensed the spirit of the mushroom inside of you, is very strong, and depending on the type of fungi, it can be unpredictable, pushing you from one state to another, from one dimension of perception to the next. The visuals are organic, morphing one into the other, bringing on visions of the vegetal earth and creatures from our mythology. On the contrary, when taking an artificially synthesized compound, the sensation is very different, and the simplest way to describe it is more digital in appearance.

The LSD visuals are not as strong as with mushrooms or DMT. They seem to be an enhancement of reality, as hallucinations are almost none or not the hyper science-fiction type that you experience with DMT when travelling the worlds of planets or the visceral kind of shrooms. With LSD, you see the subtle definition of the matrix within the images of vibrations. In this, MDMA is unique as it lacks the visuals; you don't see mandalas or dragons, no supernatural beings, and not much transformations from the normal visual perception, just a better focus and overall clarity. It is worth mentioning that MDMA is neither a psychedelic nor an amphetamine but something in between.

Looking from a more generic point of view, we can say the trip on LSD is similar to that of one induced by the magic mushrooms, in terms of length and intensity, as well as the type of energy and rhythm it sustains. LSD is the most active and energetic of them all, keeping you alive and alert, indifferent of an uplifting or bad tripping vibe. DMT is the shortest, lasting only 15 minutes, compared to the few hours that you experience on any of the other three, depending on the dose. It's also the fastest to take effect, plunging you in hyperspace moments after administration, whereas the others take at least half an hour to start.

With DMT, although you have an awakened consciousness, the awareness of the space you find yourself in is completely lost as you get transported to completely surreal dimensions, while lying in some kind of immobile trance. Mushrooms can have such a profoundly grounding effect in high doses, incapacitating your motion and putting you in an introspective state where your travels are exclusively within.

LSD can turn out both ways; it can either send your attention within or make you literally jump and embrace reality when you find yourself in nature, igniting a different sense of perceiving the textures of grass and trees, as they breathe in fascinating visual expressions, feeling the fresh smell of flowers and the way all these senses interfere with one another. MDMA is also rather malleable, as on a high dose, you'd want to lie down and take the process within, but when taking less, you're left with enough energy to feel the love of the universe while walking around with few impediments.

LSD, DMT, MDMA, as well as magic mushrooms are psychotropic substances that alter the normal way in which you perceive reality by opening your perspective to see the depthness and multidimensionality. They all establish the connection with the intricate nature of the universe, with the wilderness of the world, and with your true self, enabling you to contain and experience the whole of your being and thus the complexity of life. As such, their after-effects and what is considered their healing potential are the senses of awareness and clarity of a more sustainable self-acceptance and self-confidence of meaning and, have the remarkable result of generating beneficial change in one's life.

MDMA differs from all in focusing its action on the emotional plane. As an effect, it induces the sensation of love, universal love. As a matter of fact, with MDMA it's the most powerful vibration. It transcends the being, making you feel an overwhelmingly dear emotion towards all the people that are important in your life, towards life itself, towards your surroundings and those that are immediately close to you. For this reason, MDMA is especially helpful when it comes to overcoming traumas, allowing you to accept and forgive, to express compassion towards your being and the others involved.

Concerning the chemical structure and the way it interacts with our brain, all these substances have a different means, but they all interfere with the levels of serotonin and dopamine. Despite all others, DMT also has a particular character, being a naturally occurring compound in the human body. They all increase interconnectivity in the brain, outlining the complex network of our thoughts by switching patterns that are usually in standby and inducing a state of happiness and self-meaning.

In terms of toxicity, even though a synthesized chemical, LSD is the least harmful compound, interfering with your organism at minimum, while the MDMA is the most toxic of our list.

8. The future of LSD

The further exploration of lysergic acid is strongly connected with the future research on consciousness. The study of consciousness, in the form of a veritable science field, emerged with the new psychedelic era. One of the main points of interest concerning the LSD experience is its huge potential in revealing more and more about human consciousness through the experience of different states of being and perceiving.

The pioneers of the 50's and 60's praised this miraculous compound, infusing its image with all their peace, freedom and love ideals, with a belief that reality is not what the constricting social system is teaching us but an infinite beyond. Today's followers of the past memorable cultural figures igniting the psychedelic revolution are actually scientists, continuing their work in a frame that has the power to clean the reputation of LSD and proclaim its transcending potential.

The traditional world of medicine and science as a whole is accepting the peculiarities of the psychedelic experience in all its intensity, its extraordinary insights in past lives, out-of-body journeys, shifts of states bordering mental psychosis or schizophrenia, and the whole palette that the new-age devotees call 'spiritual awakening'. This opens a most promising future in therapy for lysergic acid, and hopefully, the laws will become properly permissive to allow the growth of research and experimentation.

The rising interest in LSD coincides with a new revival of the spiritual movement that also began in the hippie period with the Western import of Eastern practices and their integration in processes of self-development. All these drives point to an acute crisis of the world today, a crisis of individuality, as well as one of the community, a necessity to contain the ancestral wisdom of our predecessors that held a special connection with nature and their true selves, while integrating it in the understanding and routine of modern society.

A strong need to rediscover the spiritual nature of life and reality is reflected in the enthusiasm that mystic materials present to an ever wider spectrum of population, like divination methods, tarot, astrology, numerology, and a variety of other old sciences that reappear in new forms. The culture of psychedelics, and of LSD implicitly, not only rides the same wave, but also offers a gateway to the source where all these answers can be found, along with the deeper insights of the universe that we don't even know how to address yet.

We can also discuss the influence that LSD, as well as other psychedelics, have on the trend of raving people that consume drugs recreationally at parties. Although LSD can be found on the list of party drugs, a veritable experience on lysergic acid is strong enough to produce a shift consciousness such as to pursue a path of awareness, where you create an addiction. One's behavior and attachments are profoundly transformed in a way that he compassionately accepts himself and the world in its entire complexity, the good along with the bad, and this makes a person much less vulnerable, more confident, and persevering on the track that he finds meaningful for his life. As a consequence, the use of LSD has the potential to stop the abuse of psychotropic substances, replacing it with a longing of further learning and discovery.

The microdosing of LSD seems to be more and more appealing, and again, it fits perfectly on the typology of today's society. Even though the practice does not reach the level of mysticism that those on a spiritual path might be looking for, it is nonetheless a clean and efficient therapeutic means through which people can relieve their anxiety and depression, their day to day pressure, by creating a new paradigm of perceiving reality and structuring their lives towards well-being. As it appears, the future of LSD seems prolific in many directions, and this is mostly because its intricate character matches the social diversity of the contemporary man and therefore offers a solution for a variety of its modern and not so modern needs.

The rising number of urban guides that organize private, hidden therapeutic sessions with LSD is proof of acid's incredible effects, as is its use in self-exploratory and self-treatment pursuits. More than anything, it shows that people trust the substance above the therapist, enough to bypass the law, as well as the instated fear of its dangerous potential. Not to say that these underground guides are not reliable modern shamans, because most of them are doing it as they truly believe in its positive effects and consider their mission and vocation to share these beautiful experiences with others in need.

The money they receive for this service couldn't stand for a sufficient reason in this case, because they have to go through an ordeal to hide their profession and construct a different clandestine persona. If you read through the internet, you can find stories of such guides, inquiries that, of course, keep their identity secret, and discover that they are all normal people. They're not new-age hippies going to festivals, wearing tribal outfits, and promoting enlightenment; on the contrary, they're dressed in suits and spend their days in offices like the majority of us.

LSD is, for them, a means to evolve their beings. Even though they don't give acid to people at a campfire doing incantations, they know well enough how to show respect to the substance and to ensure the perfect set and setting, so their sessions are the equivalent of modern rituals, taken with the precaution of concealment. Their clients are normal people, taking their chances because they believe in the testimonies of people that had taken it before and have received precious insights that helped them change their lives for the better.

As it's seen, LSD is gaining a good reputation and credibility on the streets, not only used recreationally but therapeutically, and without the aid of legal or medical institutions, without too much research or writing available that could establish its trustworthy image, with only word of mouth and the belief in people's stories. In this line of thought, LSD seems to have a promising future independent of conventional mainstream efforts in this direction.

9. LSD - the psychedelic remedy of the modern man

If you are looking to start psychedelic therapy, LSD appears as the substance that's most friendly to begin with. It's not controllable. You have to release control so as not to be trapped in a loop and unable to take advantage of the benefits of the experience, but it is introducing you to other dimensions of thought, distorting the vision of reality without exhibiting a different existence altogether. The trip lies in the discovery of different new possibilities, lying at hand, to experience the very world we live in. The lack of strong hallucinations gives the feeling that what you see is not in fact a distortion, but an enhancement.

This book is not meant to be promotional material for LSD; rather, its purpose is to present and explain, as factually as possible, the fascination and praise that is continually growing around this psychedelic substance. The image of a drug that has the potential of abuse doesn't stand so firmly against the myriads of positive enlightening testimonials or against the psychedelic nature of LSD. Considering that an abusive user would only have part of bad trips, one would have virtually no reason to engage in such a way of consumption. The LSD journeys are such powerful, transformational experiences that is actually hard to believe that a human being can take one after the other, the way it happens with drugs that offer instant relief or glimpse of ecstasy, like amphetamines or recreational drugs.

One of the most important aspects when taking acid, or any other psychedelic, is the intention that you start with. This is an essential part of the inner setting that one has to prepare before the actual experience. The intention gives the direction of the whole journey, and if it is healing a past trauma or discovering your own spirituality, that is where LSD will take you.

Any intention that is not compatible with your being or with the nature of this substance will be impeded from the beginning and gifted with a bad trip. Reading and hearing what people have to say about it, you may notice that the ones that took acid just to have more fun but had a horrific bad trip are mentioning it as the sole experience they had on LSD. This is very different than reliving past tormenting issues or the confrontations with your own darkside that one should expect when pursuing a process of healing traumas, because in these cases, the experience is assumed from the start, and the whole journey is therapy on fast forward. Thus, LSD is the modern equivalent of the ancient trance plant medicines, a substance to fit and treat the most troubling problems of the modern man.

www.ingramcontent.com/pod-product-compliance
Lightning Source LLC
Chambersburg PA
CBHW071324080526
44587CB00018B/3339